GLORIOUS TREASURES
Ancient Egypt

First published in Great Britain in 1997 by
Brockhampton Press,
20 Bloomsbury Street,
London WC1B 3QA
A member of the Hodder Headline Group

ISBN 1 86019 564 4

A copy of the CIP data is available upon request from the
British Library.

Produced for Brockhampton Press by Flame Tree Publishing,
a part of The Foundry Creative Media Company Ltd,
The Long House, Antrobus Road, Chiswick, London W4 5HY

GLORIOUS TREASURES
Ancient Egypt

Karen Sullivan
with Penny Clarke

BROCKHAMPTON PRESS

Contents

Introduction

The ancient Egyptians developed one of the richest and most influential of all known civilizations. The valley of the River Nile, the home of this civilization, is naturally fertile, thanks to the river's annual flood. The climate is not too extreme and the neighbouring deserts provide protection from enemies. Scholars date the beginning of the flowering of the ancient Egyptian civilization to about 3200 BC, when the kingdoms of Upper and Lower Egypt were united under one ruler, the pharaoh Menes. Egypt was finally absorbed by the Romans, becoming a province of their empire in 30 BC.

This long period is usually divided by scholars into three principal periods: the Old Kingdom from 2686 to 2181 BC, the Middle Kingdom from 2133 to 1786 BC and the New Kingdom from 1567 to 1080 BC. These periods were the times of the Egyptian empire's greatest strength and richness. The times between were less settled, for the wealth of the Egyptians attracted envy and invaders, and not all the pharaohs were strong rulers or ruthless military leaders.

Today, so many thousands of years later, we still marvel at the legacy of this incredible people: the intricacy of their jewellery, the amazing quality of the carving and the confidence that caused the building – and the skill that led to the survival – of their pyramids and temples.

Coffin belonging to Imeneminet. It is decorated with gods, birds and hieroglyphs, and dates from c. 800 BC.

11

Stopper from a Canopic Urn

*To speak the name of the dead is to make them live again, and
restores the breath of life to him who has vanished.*
Inscription on the tomb of Tutankhamen

utankhamen ruled from 1361 to 1352 BC. He was aged only about eighteen when
he died, and as a pharaoh of Egypt he was largely unremarkable. Tutankhamen
owes his fame today principally to the discovery of his tomb in 1922. The artefacts
from the tomb, including this exquisite alabaster stopper, used to cork one of the
canopic jars (the four jars in which the internal organs of a deceased person were
placed) are on display at the National Museum in Cairo. Each canopic jar was
dedicated to one of the four gods of the underworld, and their stoppers were made
in the shape of a head.

*Alabaster stopper from one of the canopic jars found in the tomb of Tutankhamen,
in the shape of the pharaoh's head.*

Tutankhamen's Gold Mask

May thy Ka live! Mayest thou spend millions of years,
O thou who lovest Thebes, seated with thy face turned to the
north wind and thine eyes contemplating felicity.
Inscription on the tomb of Tutankhamen

This magnificent piece is the funeral mask of Tutankhamen. It is believed to be a portrait of the young pharaoh, and is the finest mask of its kind ever found. Made of solid gold inlaid with semi-precious stones and glass paste, the eyes and eyebrows are decorated with lapis-lazuli. The cobra and the vulture, adorning the forehead of the mask, represent the kingdoms of Upper and Lower Egypt, and were symbols of the pharaoh's power.

Funeral masks were placed on the bandaged face of a mummy. As befitted a pharaoh, Tutankhamen's mummy, with the mask in place, was put into a coffin in the shape of the mummy. This coffin was put into another, slightly larger coffin which was, itself, put into a third. The process was then repeated, but this time the large coffin, with the two smaller ones inside it, was put into a magnificent gold shrine. This shrine was put into another, which was put into another which was put into a fourth. Then the outer shrine (with the three smaller ones and the three coffins inside it) was put into a stone sarcophagus.

Confronted by the impressive workmanship of this mask, which was made for a relatively minor pharaoh, we can only wonder about those that were made for rulers such as Rameses II, lost over the years to tomb robbers.

Tutankhamen's funeral mask, probably the most beautiful of the treasures found
when his tomb was discovered in 1922.

Tutankhamen's Miniature Sarcophagi

You live again, you live again forever,
here you are young once more for ever.
Final phrase of the mummification ritual

he alabaster canopic chest found in Tutankhamen's tombhas four compartments, each of which contained a miniature gold sarcophagus inlaid with carnelian and glass paste. The four compartments were then sealed by a lid in the form of the pharaoh's head. Archeologists believe that this head is in the image of Tutankhamen, who is wearing the royal head-dress adorned with the vulture of Upper Egypt and the cobra of Lower Egypt. On his chin is the false beard worn by all pharaohs, and in his hands are the flail and the crook, two more symbols of royalty. The sarcophagus is made of pure gold, and is about 39 cm (15 in) in height. The arms and shoulders are enveloped by the wings of the protective goddesses, and the remainder of the case is decorated with a feather-like motif. On the inside of the lid is a picture of the goddess Nephthys, and the rest of the interior of this exquisite treasure is covered with magical inscriptions.

Canopic jars were so named after Canopus, pilot of the Greek king Menelaus. According to legend, he was buried at Canopus, in Egypt, and was worshipped there in the form of a jar. Early Egyptologists believed that the presence of these jars gave some credibility to the legend.

The mummification ritual was very elaborate. To prepare a corpse, the lungs, stomach, intestines and liver were removed from the body – leaving only the heart; it was believed that the gods would revive these organs and reunite them with the body to allow rebirth. When the organs were removed, the abdomen was filled with crushed myrrh, cassa and other aromatic substances, after being thoroughly cleaned with palm wine.

Above and overleaf: Miniature sarcophagus found in the tomb of the pharaoh Tutankhamen, made of gold and measuring 39 cm in height.

17

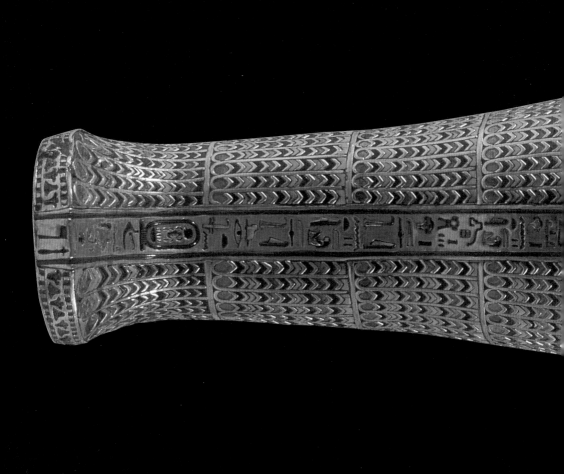

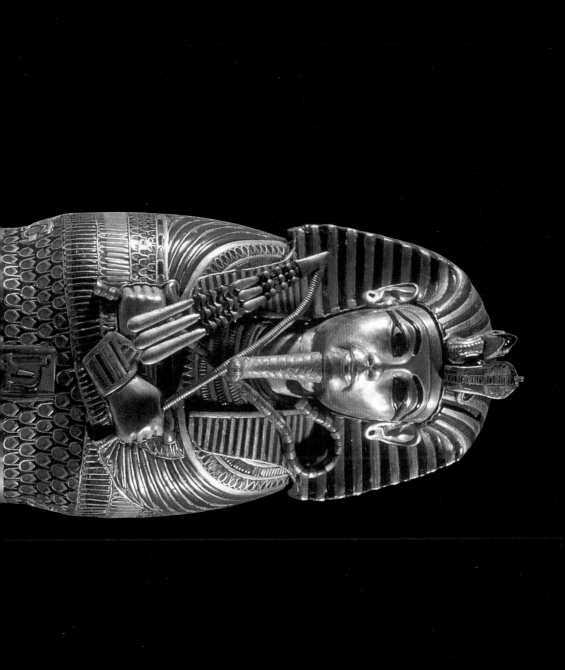

Decorated Fragment of Gold Sheet

*Behold, the king is at the head of the gods and is provided as a
god … the gods do obeisance when meeting the king just as
the gods do obeisance when meeting the rising of Ra when he
ascends from the horizon.*

Pyramid texts

This inscribed gold plate is believed to have formed part of the exterior of the gold-plated shrine created for Tutankhamen. The shrine is decorated in relief with scenes depicting the young pharaoh and his wife (the pharaoh Akhenaton's third daughter Ankhesenamun). The scenes on the double door of the shrine are surrounded by friezes, royal cartouches and birds symbolizing vassals paying homage to the pharaoh. When Tutankhamen's shrine was discovered, it contained an empty pedestal inscribed with the pharaoh's name, which suggests that its contents were pillaged. Shrines like this are known to have been assembled in an antechamber to the 'golden room' (the western chamber of a tomb) according to a set ritual. When this ritual was complete, the shrine was sealed. This happened immediately prior to the priests leaving the tomb. When the shrine had been sealed, masons erected a mud-brick wall to separate the golden room from the antechamber.

*Gold sheet fragment from Tutankhamen's grave showing a central panel of the coronation
of the pharaoh being supported by Atum and Re.*

Sandstone Relief of a Pharaoh

The old kings slumber in their pyramids,
Likewise the noble and the learned, but some
Who builded tombs have now no place of rest …
'Lay of the Harper'

The Egyptians used a particular type of relief called low relief, in which the black surface is allowed to remain as background and the figures are carved as convex projections within deeply incised outlines, although they never project beyond the surface of the rock. During the Old Kingdom (2686–2181 BC), the stylistic conventions that characterize Egyptian art were developed, notably the law of frontality, in which the human figure is represented with the eye and shoulders in front view, and the head, pelvis, legs and feet in profile. During the New Kingdom (1567–1080 BC), there was a flowering of relief sculpture, mainly in sandstone. An outline drawing was made by a draughtsman under the supervision of a master sculptor, and then specialist stone-cutters would take over with their chisels and rubbers in order to complete the relief. Mistakes were corrected in plaster.

This sandstone relief showing a pharaoh making an offering dates from c. 2nd century BC. The sa sign (protection) can be seen to the right.

Coffins of Tamoutnefret

'Tis naught
That ages, empires and religions there
Lie buried in the ravage they have wrought;
For such as he can lend – they borrow now.
Akhenaton, Pharaoh of Egypt (c.1372 –1354 BC)

For three thousand years the Egyptians embalmed their dead. The embalming process took seventy days, during which time the coffin-makers worked to create a handsomely painted coffin, with a human face. Before embalming, the body was measured, and allowance made for the bandages, so that the inner coffin would fit the mummy exactly. The shrouded mummy was usually placed in two cases of cedar, or of cloth stiffened with glue. The outer case was often covered with paintings and hieroglyphics telling of the life and various deeds of the deceased. A moulded mask of the dead person, or a portrait on linen or wood sometimes decorated the head of the case. This double case was placed in an oblong coffin; the coffin was put into a sarcophagus. A solid face, carved out of hard wood, and thought to bear an idealized resemblance to the dead person, was attached to the cover of the coffin with wooden pegs.

Painted wood coffins of Tamoutnefret, showing the various stages of encasement of the mummified body.

Coffin of Madja

Rising in thy forms as the living Aton,
Shining afar off and returning …
All eyes see thee before them.
Griffiths (Egyptologist)

his coffin was made about a hundred years before the reign of the pharaoh Tutankhamen, and its stark outline and sparse detail indicate it is the coffin of a nobleman, or middle-ranking member of the ruling class. The symbolic eye, the *ut'at*, which appears near the top, represents the sun and the moon, and often means 'to be in good health, safe, preserved and happy'. This was equally applicable to the dead and the living, since the Egyptians believed that the dead would be reborn soon after death. Whoever was preserved in the coffin would be safe and happy under the protection of the eye of Ra. The paintings on the coffin represented scenes from the life of the deceased, and the preparations for the funeral.

Painted wood coffin of Madja, an Egyptian nobleman, c. 1480 BC, decorated with scenes from the life of the deceased and the symbolic eye.

Seated Bronze Figure of Sekhmet

Kindly is she as Bast, terrible is she as Sekhet.

Philae text

he ancient Egyptians' religion was very complex. Its most striking feature was the vast number of gods and goddesses who could be represented in human, animal or other forms, and were also frequently interchangeable. Sekhmet, also known as Sekhet, was a leonine deity, symbolizing fire and the heat of the sun, and sometimes called the sun goddess, as well as an Egyptian 'Great Mother' spirit. As the conqueror of the enemies of the Egyptian gods, Sekhmet usually carried a knife, for it was she who, under the name of the 'Eye of Ra', began the task of destroying mankind. In this figure, the knife is missing. In later years, Sekhmet was known as the goddess of plagues. However, as Bastet, a cat-faced goddess, she had a much kinder nature, probably reflecting the important parts cats played in controlling vermin, such as mice and rats. Sekhmet was the consort of Ptah, the creator god of Memphis (an early capital city of Egypt and near present-day Cairo).

Seated figure of Sekhmet, the lion headed goddess, made from bronze with gold inlaid eyes and dating from c. 6th–4th century BC.

Head of Amenophis II

Long on the Egyptian coast by calms confined,
Heaven to my fleet refused a prosperous wind,
No vows had we preferred, nor victim slain,
For this the gods each favouring gale restrain.
Homer, *The Odyssey*

menophis II, pharaoh of Egypt from around 1427–1394 BC, succeeded Tuthmosis III, and was said to have been a glorious warrior, whose arrows pierced several copper targets, and who mastered a lion which surrendered like a lamb in his hands. His glories are recalled on a shield found in Tutankhamen's tomb. Amenophis II's tomb was discovered in the Valley of the Kings in 1898, but his body was found in a different royal burial site. Archeologists believe that around 1000 BC, during a period of instability, priests had removed thirteen mummies, including those of Amenophis II, Sethos II, and Siptah, from their original tombs when these were looted by brigands who used the burial chambers as hideouts. This head of Amenophis II is carved from sandstone.

*Head of Amenophis II, a great warrior pharaoh, made from sandstone
and measuring 21 cm in height.*

Shabti made for Nesikhonsu

It beggar'd all description: she did lie
In her pavilion – cloth of gold of tissue –
O'er picturing that Venus where we see
The fancy out-work nature: on each side of her
Stood pretty dimpled boys, like smiling Cupids
With divers-colour'd fans, whose wind did,
To glow the delicate cheeks which they did cool.
And what they undid did.
William Shakespeare, *Antony and Cleopatra*

This small figure or 'shabti' was created around 1000 BC, at a time when the power and status of the pharaoh was in decline. There was, however, a corresponding increase in the importance of the provincial governors, many of whom commissioned fine statues and coffins. This provided employment for the artists and craftsmen who would previously have worked for the pharaoh and his high officials. This may be a plaster cast, made from a study rapidly modelled from life in clay or wax in order to catch a likeness. Blue was a difficult colour to manufacture, and 'Egyptian blue' was achieved by grinding copper, calcium and tetrasilicate, to create the ultramarine shade characteristic of much Egyptian art.

A shabti was a helper created to guide the dead into the next life. This figure was made for Nesikhonsu, first wife of the High Priest of Thebes and the superior of the Harem of the god Amun. A harem was a socially acceptable institution; ancient Egyptians did not have a marriage contract, although most noblemen had one wife, and, depending on their wealth, a number of concubines.

Shabti created for the Superior of the Harem of the god Amun, glazed in the striking
'Egyptian blue' characteristic of so much work from this era.

Faience Amulets

So Pharaoh said to Joseph, "I hereby put you in charge of the
whole land of Egypt." Then Pharaoh took his signet ring from
his finger and put it on Joseph's finger.
Genesis, 41: 42

Along with the Sphinx and the Pyramids, the brilliant blue of the ancient Egyptians' amulets is probably one of the most enduring images of that impressive civilization. The necklace and amulets in the picture, like many other small items, are made of faience. This consists of a core of quartz covered in a thin hard glaze of a material very similar to modern glass. The glaze was principally blue, but it could also be made in a variety of colours, including red, mauve and green. The craftsmen made the blue by adding compounds of copper to the ingredients for the glass glaze before firing it in their ovens. According to the quantity and type of the copper

compounds, the blue could range from an almost almond green to the deepest indigo.

Early archeologists marvelled at the lavishness with which the Egyptians used lapis lazuli in jewellery and on funerary objects. Later study showed that much of this lapis lazuli is actually coloured glass – an appropriate tribute to the skill of those craftsmen. Amulets like these are extremely difficult to date, because the style of Egyptian jewellery changed very little throughout the many centuries of the civilization.

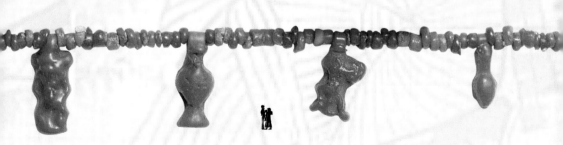

Above and overleaf: *Selection of amulets glazed in turquoise, often worn around the neck to guard against sickness and witchcraft.*

Bronze Figure of Neith

·

Hail, Great Mother, not hath been uncovered thy birth;
Hail! Great Goddess, within the underworld doubly hidden;
Thou unknown one —
Hail! thou divine one,
Not hath been unloosed thy garment.
Hymn to Neith

Neith was worshipped as a 'Great Mother' deity and was believed to be self-created and self-sustaining. She was an earth goddess who, according to the Greeks, declared to her worshippers: 'I am what has been, what is, and what shall be ...'. Her symbol was a shield and two arrows, and she is depicted with green hands and face because she was an earth spirit who provided pasture for the Egyptians' flocks. Neith has a weaver's shuttle tattooed upon her body, to indicate that it was she who provided women with their skill at the loom. This model shows Neith wearing the crown of Lower Egypt. Bronze and faience figures of this goddess are common.

Bronze figure of the goddess Neith, a 'Great Mother' deity, wearing the crown of Lower Egypt.

Bronze Head of a Cat

Cats exercise … a magic influence upon highly developed men of intellect. This is why these long-tailed Graces of the animal kingdom, these adorable, scintillating electric batteries have been the favourite animal of Mohammed, Cardinal Richlieu, Crebillon, Rousseau, and Wieland.

Leopold Von Sacher-Masoch

In ancient Egypt, cats were accepted members of every household; they were used to hunt fish and birds as well as to destroy the rats and mice that infested the grain stocks. The cat was considered so valuable that laws were passed to protect it. The Egyptians enforced strict laws prohibiting the export of cats, but because they were valued in other parts of the world, they were often smuggled out by the Greeks and Romans. Eventually a cult of cat worship developed that would last for more than two thousand years. The cat goddess Bastet (also known as Bast or Pasht) became one of the most sacred of all figures of worship. After a cat's death, its body was mummified and buried in a special cemetery. This bronze, probably a tribute to Bastet, is likely to date from the period archeologists call the Middle Kingdom, around 2133 to 1786 BC. It would have been cast in bronze round a clay core. Bronze was expensive, so figures like these were hollow.

Hollow cast bronze head of a cat. Cats were protected and venerated in ancient Egypt.

Horus the Falcon

Gods and men before the face of the gods, are weeping for thee
at the same time when they behold me!
Lo! I invoke thee with wailing that reachest high as heaven –
Yet thou hearest not my voice …
'The Burden of Isis'

In ancient Egypt, Horus was known as the sky god, sun god, and god of light and goodness. The son of Osiris and Isis, he avenged his father's murder by defeating Set (or Seth), the god of evil and darkness. The falcon symbolizes this victory and his image became symbolic with eternal life. Horus is also usually identified with the ruling pharaoh, who represented the god's triumph over evil on earth. The temple of Edfu was dedicated to Horus, and contained vivid descriptions of the battle between Horus and Set, who took the form of a hippopotamus – one of the most feared and dangerous animals of the Nile.

Bronze figure of Horus the falcon, son of Isis and Osiris, dating from c. 4th century BC.

Seated Bronze Cat

If a cat dies in a private house by a natural death,
all the inmates of the house shave their eyebrows.
Herodotus, 450 BC

ats were sacred to Bastet, and large votive figures of the cat were made of bronze and wood, often with inlaid eyes of obsidian and gold. Smaller figures, sometimes worn as amulets, were made of bronze, stone, rock-crystal and faience, and often show the cat with one or more kittens. The mother deity, Bast, is usually portrayed in this proud, seated position, and was often regarded as a form of Isis, the wife of Osiris and mother of Horus, and therefore the most important of the ancient Egyptians' female gods. The writer and historian Herodotus relates that the worship of cats in Egypt became so intense that when a house caught fire the Egyptians appeared to be most concerned about rescuing their cats, the loss of which would cause great sorrow. Anyone guilty of killing a cat would be killed – often by an angry mob.

Figure of a seated cat with pierced ears, dating from around 5th–4th century BC.

Cat and Dog Mummies

The gods gather as dogs around his feet.
Hymn to Amon-ra, the maker of men,
former of the flocks, lord of corn

Cat mummies were very common and were frequently bound with linen, in two different colours. They were placed in bronze or wooden cases made in the form of a cat, the eyes of which were inlaid with obsidian, rock-crystal or coloured paste. Wooden cat-cases were painted, and were often placed on painted pedestals. Mummified kittens were placed in rectangular bronze or wooden cases, sometimes surmounted with figures of cats. The cases containing the mummified bodies of the animals were sent to be buried at the temple of the goddess Bubastis.

Dogs were often killed deliberately and then mummified so they could be sold to pilgrims as an offering to the appropriate god or goddess. A dog features in the Egyptian myth of the Doomed Prince. Sadly, however, the papyrus scroll which tells the story is so badly damaged that no one now knows how the story ended.

Cats and dogs were mummified in much the same way as humans, with cases made of wood and linen.
These date from c. 1st century AD.

Book of the Dead

Whose names on earth are dark
But whose transmitted effluence cannot die
So long as fire outlives the parent spark …
Akhenaton, Pharaoh of Egypt (*c.*1372–1354 BC)

The *Book of the Dead* consisted of charms, spells, and formulae for use by the deceased in the afterworld. Originally inscribed on the walls of tombs, the texts were later written on papyrus rolls and frequently placed inside the mummy case. Much of what we know today about Egyptian religion is derived from these scrolls. The custom of inscribing chapters of the *Book of the Dead* upon the walls of sarcophagus chambers in the tombs can be traced back to about 2524–2400 BC; later, the practice of writing chapters of the books upon wooden coffins or sarcophagi became common, some of the texts were also inscribed upon amulets and bandages. The books (scrolls) were decorated with pictures of the gods, sacred animals, birds, mythological scenes, impressions of the funeral procession, and aspects of the life of the deceased, painted in as many as thirteen colours. The information contained in the *Book of the Dead* was intended to help the deceased overcome the foes who wished to impede his progress to rebirth. Many scrolls contain a plan of the mummy chamber and the arrangement of the furniture within.

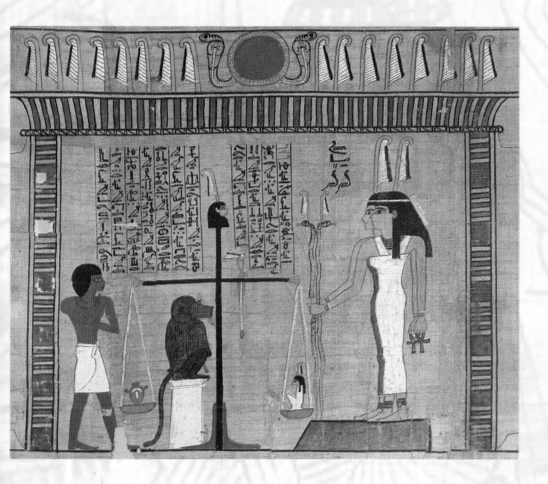

This detail from the Book of the Dead dates from around 1450 BC. Scrolls like this depicted the gods, animals and the lives of the deceased.

Nespekashuti papyrus

How manifold are all thy works,
They are hidden from before us …
Akhenaton, Pharaoh of Egypt (*c*.1372–1354 BC)

The papyrus plant is now almost extinct in Egypt but was common in antiquity. The roots were used as fuel and the pith in the stems was eaten. The stem was also used to make sandals, boats, twine, mats and cloth, and, most notably, a paper-like material. The manufacture of papyrus paper was a flourishing industry. The papyrus stems were peeled and the pith sliced into thin sections. These sections were laid side by side, then crosswise, and soaked and pressed. By beating it and then drying it, the Egyptians were able to make it into sheets of sturdy paper. Two rolls of papyrus in a box dated prior to 2700 BC, are evidence of its durability. Sheets of papyrus were joined together to produce a roll of any length, the width varying from between 15 and 43 cm (6–17 in). A roll (or 'book') of papyrus would be fastened with a length of papyrus string upon which a piece of clay was laid, impressed with a ring or scarab to form a seal. The largest Books of the Dead are 27 m (90 ft) long.

This papyrus shows Nespekashuti as a scribe. It dates from about 1000 BC. Early Egyptian tombs were largely decorated in relief, but from around 2200 BC, painting began to supersede this. Many fine Middle Kingdom (2133–1786 BC) murals have survived. The subjects are usually portrayed without specific detail and can only be identified by descriptive hieroglyphics.

Above and overleaf: *This decorated papyrus showing Nespekashuti as a scribe, dates from c. 1000 BC.*

Painted Wooden Sarcophagus

Dug from the tomb of taste-refining time,
Each form is exquisite, each block sublime.
Or good, or bad, – disfigur'd, or deprav'd, –
All art, is at its resurrection sav'd;
All crown'd with glory in the critic's heav'n,
Each merit magnified, each fault forgiven.
Sir Martin Archer Shee (Egyptologist)

The earliest Egyptian sarcophagi were made of black or green basalt, granite, agglomerate or limestone, and were rectangular with either a flat or vaulted cover. Sometime around 2100 BC, rectangular wooden coffins superseded the stone sarcophagi. This sarcophagus is a typical example dating from after 1000 BC – rounded at the head, with a human face on the cover. Most sarcophagi of this age are ornamented with rows of figures of gods, the four children of Horus, a number of genii of the afterlife and inscriptions which state that they have taken the deceased under their protection. The outstretched wings probably represent those of Isis and Nephthys and symbolize their protection of Osiris. The wooden sarcophagus would have been covered with a thin layer of gesso – a mixture of glue and whiting capable of taking a very smooth finish like a polish – and painted in rich colours.

This gesso-painted wooden sarcophagus is from the tomb of an unknown woman.
It dates from the 19th–20th dynasties.

Wooden Panel from a Sarcophagus

Awaken, O sick one, thou who hast slept,
They have lifted thine head toward the horizon.
Appear! Thou art justified against him who sought to harm thee;
Ptah has overthrown thine enemies and has ordered
Him who stood against thee to be pursued.
Thou art Horus, son of Hathor,
He whose head was restored to him after it had been cut off;
Never again shall thine head be taken from thee;
In the future never again for all eternity shall thine head be taken from thee.
Address to the dead

During the Middle Kingdom (2133–1786 BC), a school of painters flourished at Bershah. They painted wooden sarcophagi in delicate enamel-like colours with minutely detailed figures, objects and hieroglyphs. The paintings normally portrayed vivid pictures of everyday life. The inside and outside of the vaulted cover would be painted in gaudy colours, with figures of the gods, occasionally signs of the zodiac, and hieroglyphic inscriptions. The mummies belonging to such coffins were covered with a linen cloth on which was painted the god Osiris with the features of the deceased, wearing a crown and holding the flail and the crook, which symbolize royalty.

This brightly painted wooden panel shows a standing figure of Osiris, holding a crook and flail.
Above him is depicted a winged sun flanked by two soul birds.

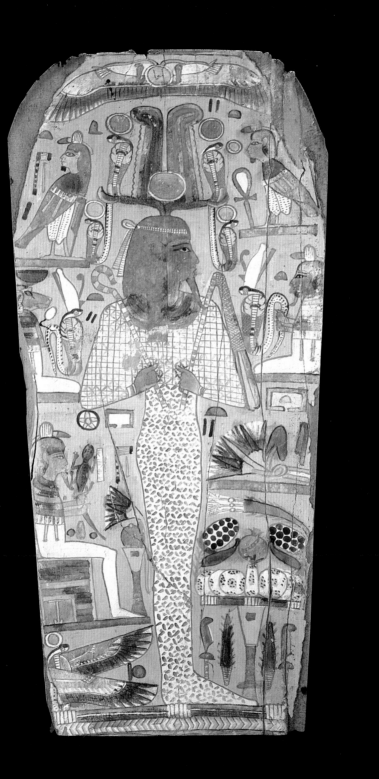

Painted Stele

Hear not the cry of mourners at the tomb,
Which have no meaning to the silent dead …
Then celebrate this fetal time, nor pause –
For no man takes his riches to the grave;
Yea, none returns again when he goes hence.
'Lay of the Harper'

Stelae are stone or terracotta slabs, usually oblong, and set upright. Used as votives or memorials, they were commonly carved with inscriptions and designs. Stelae were often used as commemorative stones in ancient Egypt, and provide a great deal of information about the life of the deceased. During the reign of Akhenaton, ancestral busts that had protected the royal Egyptian household were replaced by small shrines built in the main room of the house or in the garden. The most prominent feature of these shrines were the stelae, which showed the royal family engaged in what appear to be mainly domestic chores. However, the seemingly innocent activities of the family have a much deeper religious significance, illustrating the acts of a Holy Family who are the obvious intermediaries between man and the supreme gods (usually the sun god). The bright colours of this stele are painted on gesso (see page 54).

Gesso-painted wooden stele showing the deceased Neskhonsu.
The three lines of hieroglyphs bear an invocation to Osiris.

Wooden Coffin Cover

O King, my lord, I draw nigh to life's end,
to me the frailties of life have come
… Ah! the old lie down …
Ptah-hotep, *The Instruction*

This wooden coffin cover is carved in light relief, and probably dates from around 2000 BC. Coffins from this period were usually rectangular, with the cover consisting of one flat plank about 7.5 cm (3 in) thick. The covers were usually roughly hewn, and decorated with paintings consisting of large stripes of blue, red, green and yellow, interspersed with well-cut hieroglyphics. Both the inside and the outside of the cover were usually inscribed with symbols from the *Book of the Dead*. Often there were extraordinarily profuse decorations with rows of amulets, all painted in the most vibrant colours and covered with a bright varnish. Coffins were closed by dowels, through which pegs of wood were driven. These were covered with plaster and painted, making them invisible. After about 900 BC, the art of coffin-making degenerated and work became rough and careless, leading to the end of the practice of mummification and burial that was such an intrinsic part of Egyptian culture.

This wooden coffin cover dates from c. 2000 BC. It shows the bright colours of painted hieroglyphs and symbols from the Book of the Dead.

Wooden Female Sarcophagus

… King of Kings;
Look on my works, ye mighty, and despair.
Khufu

Many of the sarcophagi dating from between 2180 and 2035 BC are beautifully sculpted. Some had their sides made to represent the openings and doors of the mastabas (tombs with sloping sides and a flat roof), and the inscriptions normally only recorded the names and titles of their owners, and prayers that sepulchral gifts would be made to the deceased on specified festival dates. The wealth of the Egyptian civilization declined at this time, and with it the number of fine tombs commissioned from artists and craftsmen. Tombs of wood replaced those of granite or fine limestone and the demand for funerary arts died out almost completely. Fortunately, with the return of prosperity, the demand for funereal work was revived.

Lid of a plain wooden sarcophagus, found in a woman's tomb and dating from the late period, c. 6th century BC.

Pendant of Rameses II

Bright is the earth when thou riseth in the horizon,
When thou shinest as Aton by day.
The darkness is banished, when thou sendest forth thy rays ...
Akhenaton, Pharaoh of Egypt (*c*.1372–1354 BC)

Rameses II (reigned 1292-1225 BC) usurped the throne from his brother, and was probably the pharaoh who enslaved the Hebrews as described in the *Old Testament*. Under his rule Egypt acquired unprecedented splendour, the empire extending from southern Syria to the fourth cataract of the Nile. He left monuments throughout Egypt, notably at Karnak, Luxor, Thebes and Abu Simbel. The period was characterized by great luxury, increased slavery and the growth of a mercenary army – all contributors to Egypt's eventual decline.

The Egyptians' command of the applied arts shows their appreciation of form and beauty. The standard of metal working was high, and fine vessels, pendants and jewellery of all forms were produced. Much use was made of gilded decoration, sometimes on a base of modelled gesso, and Egyptian faience (glazed quartz) was commonly used for beads and inlays. When producing jewellery, a workshop's head goldsmith would weigh the metal that was brought from the sands of the eastern desert, then workers would cast, solder and fit together exquisitely detailed treasures. This pendant is inlaid with semi-precious stones and silver, which was very rare in ancient Egypt. The outspread wings may symbolize the protection of the four goddesses or it may represent the vulture goddess of the South. The serpent goddess of the North appears at the bottom of the pendant. Tutankhamen had an exquisite vulture pendant which may have inspired Rameses to commission something similar for himself.

Above and overleaf: *Gold and silver pendant belonging to Rameses II, dating from c. 1270 BC. This was probably inspired by a similar vulture pendant belonging to Tutankhamen.*

65

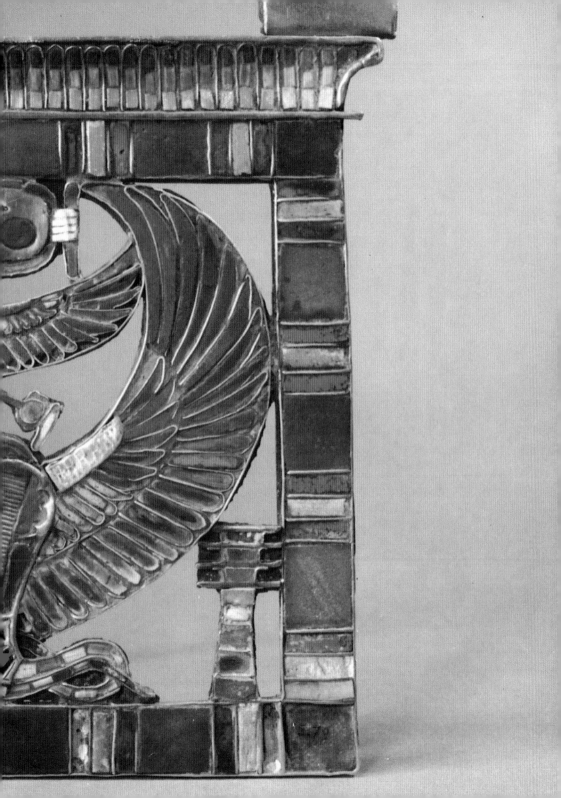

Striding Bronze Figure

I met a traveller from an antique land
Who said: Two vast and trunkless legs of stone
Stand in the desert. Near them, on the sand,
Half sunk, a shattered visage lies, whose frown,
And wrinkled lip, and sneer of cold command.
Tell that its sculptor well those passions read
Which yet survive, stamped on these lifeless things.
The hand that mocked them and the heart that fed;
And on the pedestal these words appear:
'My name is Ozymandias, king of kings:
Look on my works, ye mighty, and despair!'
Nothing beside remains. Round the decay
Of that colossal wreck, boundless and bare,
The lone and level sands stretch far away.
Percy Bysshe Shelley, 'Ozymandias'

This striding pharaoh is wearing a pleated kilt and what may be the Red Crown, which was the headdress of the pharaoh of Lower Egypt. This statuette (*c.* 2100 BC), was probably one of many mass-produced at this time from heavily leaded bronze. Most of those that have survived are covered with a green patina, but they would originally have been burnished to resemble gold. Some may have been covered with a thin layer of gesso. Metalwork, as opposed to carving, allowed the artist to create bent arms and drill holes through clenched hands to hold staffs and sceptres. Statues could assume the postures of figures represented in the two-dimensional art which adorned the tomb walls.

Figure of a pharaoh, made of bronze with his left hand raised
– probably to hold a staff which is now missing.

Linen-bound Mummy

Glory from those who made the world their prey;
And he is gathered to the kings of thought
Who waged contention with their time's decay,
And of the past are all that cannot pass away.
Akhenaton, Pharaoh of Egypt (*c.*1372–1354 BC)

Although the word 'mummy' means any body that has been embalmed before burial, it is usually used to refer to ancient Egyptian burials. There the dry air preserved the embalmed and tightly wrapped bodies for over five thousand years. Royal figures, their retinue, and even food, were preserved. Preparations were made for eternal life, according to rites established at a stage in Egyptian history known as

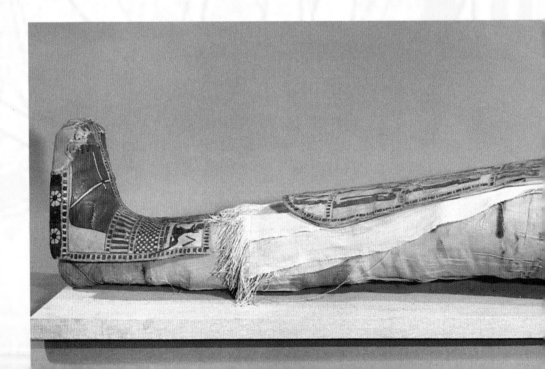

the 'time of the gods'. The embalming workshop was called 'The House of Vigour', and the process of embalming could be called the restoration of vitality. The internal organs were extracted from the body for storage in canopic jars, and the body was shaved and packed for a period of seventy days in natron, a natural salt that absorbed all the body's moisture. The dried-out body was then bandaged with lengths of fine linen (although cotton was sometimes used), and during this process prayers were recited and magic formulae pronounced while oils and ointments were poured over the strips of cloth. Mummy cloths were usually plain, although texts from the *Book of the Dead* were occasionally painted on them. The face was often covered by a mask, and the mummy (in the case of men of wealth) covered with treasures. In the tomb, the mummy was placed with its head to the West and feet to the East so that when the dead came back to life, they would be facing the rising sun.

Mummy bound in linen, clearly showing the decorated mask used to cover the head of the mummified body.

Amenemhet II as a Sphinx

Choice victims in the temples of the gods;
He who goes Yonder is a learned man,
Whom no one hinders when he calls to Ra.
Egyptian poem

The Sphinx, a mythical beast of ancient Egypt, is usually represented with a human head and a lion's body. It frequently symbolized the pharaoh as an incarnation of the sun god Ra, as does this sphinx of Amenemhet II. The most famous is the Great Sphinx, a colossal stone figure built by the pharaoh Chephren around 2200 BC. Amenemhet I (d. 1970 BC), pharaoh of Egypt and founder of the twelfth dynasty that began the Middle Kingdom, around 2133 BC, centralized the country's government. The strength of the dynasty enabled arts and science to flourish. His son, Amenemhet II sent men south to Nubia to dig for gold and he opened the mines in the valley of Hammamat. Exquisite jewellery has been found at Dashur, where Amenemhet II and his grandson Senusert III lived and built their pyramids. Many tombs were guarded by two sphinxes, or 'guardian lions'.

Pharaoh Amenhemet II portrayed in the form of a sphinx. This carving is from granite and dates from c. 1900 BC.

Hathor and Seti 1st

For the angel of death spread his wings on the blast,
And breathed in the face of the foe as he passed …
Lord Byron, *'The Destruction of Sennacherib'*

t is Seti I, son and successor of Rameses I, who is commemorated in this bas-relief. Many scholars believe that Seti I oppressed the Jews, and that his son Rameses II (ruled 1292–1225 BC) was the pharaoh of the Hebrew Exodus. Judging from contemporary art, Seti was a tall, intelligent man and his name appears on shrines all over Egypt. This bas-relief was carved about 600 years after his death. He was an excellent warrior, and he built a great sanctuary to Osiris at Abydos. Hathor was the goddess of joy and love, of the sky, and of the West – the abode of the dead. Her consort was Horus, the son of Isis and Osiris. Bas-relief, also known as 'raised relief', characterizes work in which the entire background is lowered, leaving the figures and inscriptions raised. These carvings were often made into limestone blocks and brilliantly painted over with a thin coat of gesso to retain the sandstone colouring.

Coloured limestone bas-relief depicting Seti I, a great warrior pharaoh,
with Hathor, goddess of joy and love.

Coffin of Imeneminet

His kingdom passed away,
He, in the balance weighed,
Is light and worthless clay;
The shroud his robe of state,
His canopy the stone;
The Mede is at his gate!
The Persian on his throne!
Lord Byron

offins in the eighth and ninth centuries BC were painstakingly decorated with texts and images relating to rebirth and the afterlife. They were often painted with inscriptions in many colours on a white background, and the scenes on the covers were divided into two groups by perpendicular inscriptions between them. Faces on the coffins were usually flesh coloured and gilded. The eyes, often made of obsidian, were inlaid between eyelids of the same material or of bronze. Mummies of this period were protected by cases made of *cartonnage* (a form of papier-mâché), and laid in two or three coffins. The *cartonnage* cases were completely enclosed, and many mummies have never, to this day, been removed from them. Their contents, however, can be investigated by modern techniques, such as X-ray, which reveal what lies within the linen wrappings. Many coffins of this period are covered with pictures of gods and inscribed with extracts from the *Book of the Dead*. The hair surrounding the face on this coffin is in the brilliant aquamarine often referred to as 'Egyptian blue'.

Coffin belonging to Imeneminet (back and front). It is decorated with gods, birds and hieroglyphs, and dates from c. 800 BC.

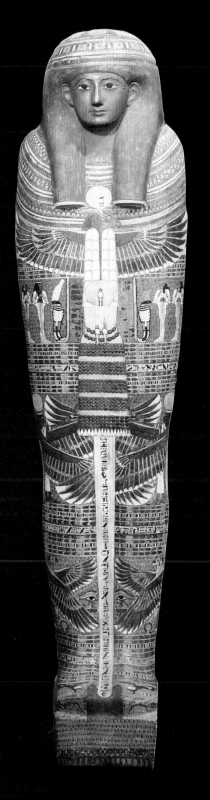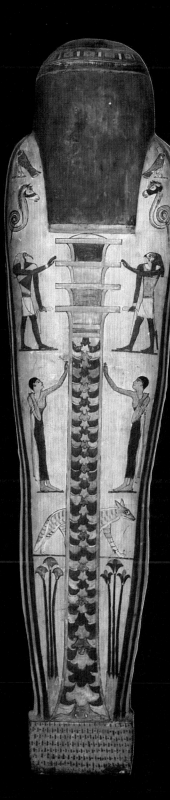

Pectoral Decoration of Isis

The bull, begotten of the two cows, Isis and Nephthys …
He, the progeny of the two cows, Isis and Nephthys,
The child surpassingly beautiful.
'The Burden of Isis'

sis was the goddess of nature whose worship, originating in ancient Egypt, gradually extended throughout the lands of the Mediterranean and became one of the chief religions of the Roman Empire. The worship of Isis, together with that of her brother and husband, Osiris, and their son, Horus, resisted the rise of Christianity and lasted until the sixth century AD. Isis was the ideal woman, wife and mother. When her husband, Osiris, was killed and the pieces of his body scattered throughout all four corners of the earth, Isis roamed the world, collecting every piece of him, so that Osiris could be restored to life again. She also conceived Horus, posthumously, which makes her an important figure in rebirth and the netherworld. The figure of Isis appears on coffins from all periods of ancient Egyptian history, and it forms a religious pattern of purity – Isis's wings are often interlaced with those of Nephthys. The four protecting goddesses are Isis, Nephthys, Neith and Serket, and their faces are usually turned sideways to emphasize their vigilant attitudes and caring expressions. Their winged arms usually spread around the burial receptacle as a symbol of protection.

Pectoral decoration in the form of a winged Isis, dating from c. 1000 BC.
Made from turquoise-glazed composition

Gold Ring

And there lay the steed with his nostril all wide,
But through it there rolled not the breath of his pride;
And the foam of his gasping lay white on the turf,
And cold as the spray of the rock-beating surf.

And there lay the rider distorted and pale,
With the dew on his brow, and the rust on his mail:
And the tents were all silent — the banners alone —
The lances unlifted — the trumpet unblown.
Lord Byron, 'The Destruction of Sennacherib'

The Hyksos (north-western Semitic peoples who conquered Egypt around 1786 BC) were responsible for introducing the horse into Egypt, which largely contributed to the later military success of the Egyptians. From 1860 BC, the time when this ring was made, charioteers in action are depicted on monuments and other art forms. This fine gold ring is characteristic of the period, with the gold accentuated by the brilliant carnelian. Ancient Egyptian jewellery often used both colourful beads and motifs, such as the scarab, and because the horse played an important part in their military successes, it took on a symbolism which can be seen in much art of this period.

Gold rings were worn by anyone of wealth, and they were placed on the fingers of the deceased after the mummification process.

Fine gold ring inlaid with carnelian, and decorated with two prancing horses.
These were symbolic of Egyptian military success.

Head of Nectanebo II

Egypt, thou knew'st too well
My heart was to thy rudder tied by the strings,
And thou should'st tow me after.
William Shakespeare, *Antony and Cleopatra*

This head of a pharaoh is carved from green basalt, and dates from around 350 BC. The pharaoh wears a crown displaying the symbols of his power: the asp and the vulture. Its date suggests that this is probably a portrait of the pharaoh Nectanebo II who ruled from 359 to 341 BC. Although the head is damaged it is nevertheless a powerful portrait.

One of the last of the Eyptian pharaohs, much of Nectanebo II's reign (and that of his predecessor Nectanebo I) was spent in fending off attacks by the Persians. To try to stop the encroachment of forces under the Persian ruler, Xerxes III, Nectanebo formed alliances with the Greek city-states, in particular Sparta. Eventually, however, he was forced to flee after successful Persian campaigns.

When not involved in defending his empire's boundaries, Nectanebo II undertook a massive building programme. He was responsible for the huge halls and gateways that enclose the temples built by many earlier pharaohs. These constructions are still standing today. The extent of this building, and the number of labourers such a task would have required, are indications of the continuing wealth of the Eygptian empire. Only a state that was enormously rich could undertake such work while having to defend its frontiers against the attacks of an enemy as persistent as the Persians.

Green basalt head of a pharaoh, attributed to Nectanebo II, the last ruler of the 30th dynasty in Egypt.

Bronze Figure of the Goddess Wadjet

*'I have had to rely on the accounts given to me by the Egyptians
and their priests. They have told me that 341 generations separate
the first King of Egypt from the last and that there was
one King and one High Priest to each generation.
Reckoning three generations as a century … a total of 11,340 years.'*
Herodotus, Book II, 142

Egyptian artists represented gods and goddesses in a number of different forms. This bronze figure of the goddess Wadjet, the cobra goddess of Lower (northern) Egypt, is shown with the body of a woman and the head of a lioness. The cobra itself rears out from the body of the goddess, its hood open. Although the Egyptian cobra is probably better known as the asp, forever linked with the death of Cleopatra, Wadjet played a more benign role. She helped save Horus, child of Isis and Osiris, from his jealous uncle Seth, who had already killed Osiris.

The goddess is wearing one of the many crowns of Egypt. It consists of a double upright plume, a pair of cow's horns in the shape of a lyre, with a disc in between them. Each element in the crowns worn by pharaohs, gods and goddesses had a special meaning. Here, the double plumes represent the sky, the disc the sun, and the horns the goddesses Hathor and Isis, both of whom were believed to have maternal, protective powers.

Lions were quite common in Egypt and North Africa before the Roman period. Unfortunately, the Romans' insatiable quest for animals to be hunted and killed (by prisoners and gladiators) in the arenas of Rome and other cities, led to their extinction in Egypt and most of the Middle East and North Africa.

Bronze figure of Wadjet, standing against an obelisk. This piece dates from c. 4th century BC.

Blue-glazed Wig

My heart thinks only of your love …
I run quickly towards you with my hair disarranged …
but I will set my curls and be ready in a moment.
Love poetry written *c*. 1500 BC

Although these words were written around 1500 BC, the sentiments behind them are timeless. Much of what remains of the ancient Egyptian civilization is so massive and magnificent it can be intimidating, which is largely how it was intended. Words like these, however, shorten the centuries, by illustrating the importance placed by the Egyptians on normal things such as hair and hairstyles. Fashions in hair changed far more than fashions in clothes. Sometimes the men wore their hair long, while women wore it short. At other times the fashions were reversed. Sometimes the hair was curled, sometimes it was plaited. On special occasions ribbons and flowers were used.

Evidence of this interest can be found in the many surviving papyri, which offer cures for baldness and recipes for lotions to prevent grey hair. Even if an Egyptian did not suffer from either of these complaints, it was custom for both men and women to wear wigs, particularly on special occasions. The wigs could be made entirely of human hair or else from a mixture of human hair and plant fibres. These hairpieces were considered so essential that when their owners died, they were put in special boxes along with other items that would be needed for life in the next world, and buried with them. The wig in this picture, however, was not created for human use; a wig such as this would have been made to grace the head of a statue.

Wig created for a statue. The colour of its glaze is the 'Egyptian Blue'
which characterizes much Egyptian jewellery and sculpture.

Scarab Amulets

Ra of the horizon who rejoices in the horizon in his name of
Ra the Father who comes in the Aton.
Rebirth chant

These two scarabs are glazed in blue. The flat underside of the top one is inscribed for use as a seal, whereas the lower scarab has its wings open, showing it was used as a funerary amulet. Amulets like this were placed between the linen bandages in which the embalmers wrapped the mummified remains of a dead person, before putting the mummy into its elaborate case.

Scarabs played an extremely significant part in the religious beliefs of the ancient Egyptians: they were believed to have magical powers and so affected all aspects of the Egyptians' lives. They also provided an enormously important practical service, for the scarab represents the dung, or burying, beetle, which does exactly what their name suggests: a pair will gather dung, roll it into a ball, excavate a hole in the sand and bury it. The female lays her eggs in the ball of dung, which provides food for the young when they emerge from the eggs. In the hot climate of Egypt, removing dung was essential in the prevention of disease.

It was the beetle's practice of rolling its ball of dung that made the Egyptians think it had magical powers. To them the ball represented the sun as it crossed the sky on its daily journey, so the scarab was often associated with the sun god, Re.

These scarabs are made from stone or faience and used as talismans by the Egyptians.
They are glazed in turquoise and bright blue.

Notes on Illustrations

Page 10 Detail from *Coffin of Imeneminet* (Louvre, Paris). Courtesy of Visual Arts Library. **Page 13** *Kanopendeckel mit Bildnis Tut-anch-Amuns* photographed by Erich Lessing (National Museum, Cairo). Courtesy of AKG. **Page 15** *Gold Mask of Tutankhamen* photographed by Erich Lessing (National Museum, Cairo). Courtesy of AKG. **Page 17** Detail from *Miniatursarg Tut-anch-Amun* photographed by Erich Lessing (National Museum, Cairo). Courtesy of AKG. **Pages 18-19** *Miniatursarg Tut-anch-Amun* photographed by Erich Lessing (National Museum, Cairo). Courtesy of AKG. **Page 21** *Decorated Gold Sheet Fragment of Tutankhamun*. Courtesy of Christie's Images. **Page 23** *Sandstone Relief of a Pharaoh*. Courtesy of Christie's Images. **Page 25** *Coffins of Tamoutnefret* (Louvre, Paris). Courtesy of Visual Arts Library. **Pages 26-7** *Coffin of Madja* (Louvre, Paris). Courtesy of Visual Arts Library. **Page 29** *Bronze Seated Figure of Sekhmet*. Courtesy of Christie's Images. **Page 31** *Head of Amenophis II* (Louvre, Paris). Courtesy of Visual Arts Library. **Page 33** *Bright Blue Glazed Composition Shabti*. Courtesy of Christie's Images. **Pages 34-5** Detail from *Selection of Turquoise Glazed Composition Amulets*. Courtesy of Christie's Images. **Pages 36-7** Detail from *Selection of Turquoise Glazed Composition Amulets*. Courtesy of Christie's Images. **Page 39** *Fine Bronze Figure of Neith Goddess*. Courtesy of Christie's Images. **Page 41** *Egyptian Hollow Cast Bronze Head of a Cat*. Courtesy of Christie's Images. **Page 43** *Egyptian Bronze Figure of Horus the Falcon*. Courtesy of Christie's Images. **Page 45** *Egyptian Bronze Figure of a Seated Cat*. Courtesy of Christie's Images. **Page 47** *Mummies of Cat and Dog* (Louvre, Paris). Courtesy of Visual Arts Library. **Page 49** *Detail from the Book of the Dead* (Louvre, Paris). Courtesy of Visual Arts Library. **Page 51** Detail from *Nespakachouti Papyrus* (Louvre, Paris). Courtesy of Visual Arts Library. **Pages 52-3** *Nespakachouti Papyrus* (Louvre, Paris). Courtesy of Visual Arts Library. **Page 55** *Gesso Painted Wooden Sarcophagus for an Unknown Lady*. Courtesy of Christie's Images. **Page 57** *Wooden Painted Panel from a Sarcophagus*. Courtesy of Christie's Images. **Page 59** *Gesso Painted Wooden Stele*. Courtesy of Christie's Images. **Page 61** *Couvercle du Cercueil de Petsoris* (Musée de Cairo). Courtesy of Visual Arts Library. **Page 63** *Wooden Female Sarcophagus Lid*. Courtesy of Christie's Images. **Page 65** Detail from *Pendant of Ramases II* (Louvre, Paris). Courtesy of Visual Arts Library. **Pages 66-7** *Pendant of Ramases II* (Louvre, Paris). Courtesy of Visual Arts Library. **Page 69** *Bronze Figure of a Striding King*. Courtesy of Christie's Images. **Pages 70-1** *Pacheri Mummy* (Louvre, Paris). Courtesy of Visual Arts Library. **Page 73** *Amenemhet II as a Sphinx* (Louvre, Paris). Courtesy of Visual Arts Library. **Page 75** *Hathor and Sethi I* (Louvre, Paris). Courtesy of Visual Arts Library. **Page 77** *Coffin of Imeneminet* (Louvre, Paris). Courtesy of Visual Arts Library. **Page 79** *Egyptian Turquoise Glazed Composition Pectoral in the Form of a Winged Isis*. Courtesy of Christie's Images. **Page 81** *Ring with Horses* (Louvre, Paris). Courtesy of Visual Arts Library. **Page 83** *Important Green Basalt Portrait Head of a Pharaoh*. Courtesy of Christie's Images. **Page 85** *Bronze Figure of Wadjet Standing Against an Obelisk*. Courtesy of Christie's Images. **Page 87** *Glazed Egyptian Blue Wig*. Courtesy of Christie's Images. *Head of Amenophis II* (Louvre, Paris). Courtesy of Visual Arts Library. **Page 89** *Bright Blue and Turquoise Glazed Composition Mummy Bead Net*. Courtesy of Christie's Images.

Index